The Ultimate Guide To The Lenovo X1 Carbon (Gen 12, 2024)

Revealing the Strategies,Tips and Tricks for Enhancing the Performance of the Laptop

By

Kevin Editions

Table Of Contents

Introduction

Lenovo's 2024 ThinkPad X1 Carbon (Gen 12) is the zenith of modern laptop design as it captures Lenovo's innovation, durability, and functionality. This version is the twelfth iteration of the iconic ThinkPad X1 Carbon line, and it represents years of fine-tuning and advancements in technology.

The Gen 12 X1 Carbon has a sleek and professional design at its core which is aimed at meeting the needs of businesspeople and power users too. The laptop's exterior boasts lightweight yet strong built that includes a combination of top-end materials such as aluminum, magnesium and aerospace grade carbon fiber. This not only allows for high durability but also ensures excellent portability making this device perfect for frequent travelers or busy professionals on the move.

Approaching its display, one unique thing about X1 Carbon Gen 12 is its remarkable graphics. It utilizes a 14-inch LCD that comes with a 16:10 aspect ratio that offers an immersive viewing experience with vivid colors and sharp details. The screen displays clear visuals for work, leisure activities, or anything in between thanks to its 2880 x 1800 pixels resolution. Whether you are editing documents or watching movies or just surfing through different web pages, thank God you will have access to X1 Carbon Display

The X1 Carbon Gen 12 boasts the latest cutting-edge Intel Core Ultra CPU under its chassis which offers unrivalled performance and power efficiency. The inclusion of an Ultra 7 155H chip running at 1.4 GHz ensures smooth multitasking, fast processing speeds and improved graphics performance. This makes it well-suited for a range of tasks such as productivity work, content creation and even some light gaming.

Connectivity wise, the X1 Carbon Gen 12 is loaded with a wide array of ports and wireless options. It has two Thunderbolt 4 USB-C ports in addition to two USB-A ports, a full-size HDMI port, and an optional SIM card slot (available). This means that users can effortlessly connect external devices, peripherals or displays thereby boosting productivity and workflow efficiency.

Also in terms of security, the X1 Carbon Gen 12 is top notch. These include sophisticated biometric identification systems like fingerprint scanning as well as manual privacy shutters on webcams. Users could also secure boot options, encryption tools, Lenovo's dynamic security software among other things.

With its efficient performance and rich feature set, the X1 Carbon Gen 12 is still remarkably thin and light, just weighing at 2.2lbs. As a result, it can be easily carried around and used in different settings such as coffee shops, meetings or on your way to work.

The Lenovo ThinkPad X1 Carbon (Gen 12, 2024) is an epitome of modern laptop innovation as it combines luxury design, high performance and advanced security features packed in a portable and stylish body. Therefore, if you are a business person; creative artist or simply love tech products then this could be the best option for you that exceed your expectation.

Chapter 1: Getting Started

Unboxing and Initial Setup

A very exciting experience is unboxing the Lenovo ThinkPad X1 Carbon (Gen 12, 2024) that sets the tone for the amazing performance and usability of this laptop. The moment you hold a slim, well-wrapped box in your hands you know you are about to see a high-end device made with great attention to detail.

Once opened, the packaging foam will reveal the actual X1 Carbon wrapped up tightly to keep it safe from harm during shipping. Slim contour and sophisticated design make it evident from first sight that Lenovo believes in minimalism as far as its products are concerned.

You will find additional items necessary for setting up and using it beside the computer. That typically includes power supply units, USB-C cables for charging or data transfer purposes and sometimes other documentations/manuals. With some configurations, Lenovo additionally offers a stylus pen which can be used for drawing, note-taking or creative tasks.

Setting up the X1 Carbon is very easy and friendly to users, which means that all you need to do is get set up as quickly as possible. On opening the laptop, connect the power adapter and charge the battery. It comes with a quick charging technology feature that ensures in no time whatsoever, your battery is full and ready to go.

Once the battery has been fully charged, turn on the laptop by pressing a power button found at either top or side of its keyboard. The computer will start booting and take you through an initial setup wizard after this. You will be asked by this wizard for your choice of language, region and keyboard layout so that it could be set according to your taste.

Afterwards, you will be required to connect to a Wi-Fi network for internet access and downloading updates. While Lenovo often loads users' machines with software applications as well as drivers designed to enhance their experience with them, make sure you check for updates during initial setup because there may be new features or fixes in place already.

When preparing, you also obtain an opportunity to create user accounts, choose security options like passwords or biometrics and personalize settings which include display preferences and system configurations. Lenovo has ensured that the setup wizard provides detailed instructions and prompts that can be understood by anyone regardless of their expertise in computers; making it easier for them to alter their X1 Carbon in a way that would suit each individual.

The X1 Carbon is now ready for use after the setup phase is complete. Be it for work purposes, entertainment or any other creative activities; this device's powerful performance, strikingly elegant screen as well as top-of-the-line construction makes its usage smooth right from when you open it out of its box until when you complete setting it up.

Overview of the Laptop's Design and Features

The style and characteristics of Lenovo ThinkPad X1 Carbon (Gen 12, 2024) are a blend of gracefulness, practicality and endurance in that business laptops world. In creating the X1 Carbon though, Lenovo has really paid attention to detail so as to satisfy the needs of contemporary professionals but without evading its iconic design elements that have made people refer to this line as the ThinkPad.

Firstly, the outside of X1 Carbon is gently curved with very clean lines which makes it look elegant. It is slim, having got a matte black cover that will make you feel like wearing an evening gown while going for an interview on Wall Street. The inclusion of such quality materials as aluminum, magnesium and carbon fibers does not only contribute towards its beauty but also adds up to its ability to last long through being light.

In terms of its robustness though X1 Carbon is considered to be top-notch due to having a strong frame which can go through daily rough handling. As part of ensuring the durability aspect for instance, this laptop should have undergone rigorous testing or it should have been certified under MIL-STD-810H so as to ensure resistance against shocks, vibrations and extreme temperatures. For professionals who are always on the move then this becomes their best friend thereby becoming reliable.

One of the standout features of the X1 Carbon's design is its portability. Weighing only 2.2 pounds and measuring 21 millimeters thick, it is very light and slim, making it easy to carry in a bag or briefcase without adding unwanted weight. Further, the laptop has got long battery life which adds to its portability thus enabling users to work on it for longer.

The laptop also comes with a high-resolution screen that provides an impressive visual experience for both work and entertainment. This device has a 14-inch LCD with 16:10 aspect ratio and resolution of 2880 x1800 pixels thereby giving clear and vibrant pictures with good color reproduction and sharpness. The X1 Carbon display brings in immersive viewing experiences regardless of whether you are editing documents, watching movies or browsing through various websites.

Regarding connections, the X1 Carbon satisfies needs modern workflow through different ports as well as wireless options. It comes with two Thunderbolt 4 USB-C ports, two USB-A ports, one full-size HDMI port and an optional SIM card slot. Therefore various displays, peripherals and accessories can be connected easily hence improving productivity as well as workflow efficiency terribly.

The keyboard and input options on the X1 Carbon are also noteworthy. The laptop's keyboard is renowned for its comfort, tactile feedback, and durability, making typing a pleasure even during long hours of use. The inclusion of a TrackPoint pointing stick and a wide touchpad provides users with multiple input options to suit their preferences and workflow requirements.

Security is a key focus of the X1 Carbon's design, with features such as biometric authentication (fingerprint reader), a webcam with a manual shutter for privacy, and encryption options to protect sensitive data. Lenovo's robust security software suite further enhances the laptop's security posture, giving users peace of mind in today's digital age.

Overall, the Lenovo ThinkPad X1 Carbon (Gen 12, 2024) excels in both design and features, offering a perfect balance of style, functionality, and durability for discerning professionals. Whether you're a business executive, creative professional, or on-the-go entrepreneur, the X1 Carbon is designed to meet your needs and exceed your expectations.

Connecting to Power and Peripherals

Connecting the Lenovo ThinkPad X1 Carbon (Gen 12, 2024) to power and peripherals is a straightforward process designed to provide users with convenience and versatility in their computing experience. Whether you're in the office, at home, or on the go, the X1 Carbon offers multiple options for powering up and connecting external devices to enhance productivity and workflow efficiency.

The X1 Carbon comes equipped with a power adapter that connects to the laptop via a USB-C port, providing fast and efficient charging capabilities. The USB-C port supports rapid charging technology, allowing users to quickly recharge the battery and get back to work without lengthy downtimes. This is especially beneficial for professionals who are constantly on the move and need a reliable power source to keep their laptop running throughout the day.

In addition to the power adapter, the X1 Carbon features a range of ports and connectors to accommodate various peripherals and accessories. The laptop includes two Thunderbolt 4 USB-C ports, which not only support high-speed data transfer but also serve as power delivery ports for charging compatible devices. This versatility allows users to connect multiple peripherals such as external displays, storage drives, and docking stations with ease.

For users who prefer traditional USB-A peripherals, the X1 Carbon also includes two USB-A ports, providing compatibility with a wide range of legacy devices and accessories. These ports can be used to connect USB flash drives, external keyboards, mice, and other

USB-enabled devices without the need for adapters or converters.

The X1 Carbon's connectivity options extend further with a full-size HDMI port, which allows users to connect the laptop to external monitors, projectors, and displays for enhanced multitasking and productivity. Whether you're giving a presentation, collaborating with colleagues, or enjoying multimedia content, the HDMI port ensures seamless connectivity and high-quality video output.

In addition to wired connections, the X1 Carbon also offers wireless connectivity options to suit modern workflow needs. The laptop features built-in Wi-Fi and Bluetooth capabilities, allowing users to connect to wireless networks, peripherals, and accessories without the need for physical cables. This wireless connectivity enhances flexibility and mobility, enabling users to work and collaborate from anywhere within range of a Wi-Fi network.

The X1 Carbon's versatility in power and peripheral connectivity makes it a versatile tool for professionals in various industries. Whether you're a business executive, creative professional, or student, the X1 Carbon's seamless integration with power sources and peripherals ensures a smooth and efficient computing experience. With its modern design, robust features, and flexible connectivity options, the X1 Carbon is designed to meet the demands of today's dynamic work environments.

Chapter 2: Using Your ThinkPad X1 Carbon

Navigating the Operating System (Windows or other)

Navigating the operating system, whether it's Windows or another system, on the Lenovo ThinkPad X1 Carbon (Gen 12, 2024) is a user-friendly and intuitive experience designed to enhance productivity and efficiency for users of all levels. The X1 Carbon comes equipped with the latest Windows operating system, offering a familiar interface with robust features and customization options. Additionally, users have the flexibility to install and navigate other operating systems based on their preferences and needs.

When you power on the X1 Carbon, you're greeted with the familiar Windows desktop environment, complete with the Start menu, taskbar, and notification center. The Start menu provides quick access to frequently used apps, documents, and settings, allowing users to launch applications and perform tasks with ease. The taskbar houses shortcuts to commonly used apps, system tools, and notifications, providing convenient access to essential functions.

One of the key features of navigating Windows on the X1 Carbon is the integration of touch and pen input. The laptop's touchscreen display and optional stylus pen allow users to interact with the operating system in a more intuitive and tactile manner. Whether you're swiping, tapping, or drawing, the touchscreen capabilities of the X1 Carbon enhance productivity and creativity, especially for tasks such as note-taking, sketching, and graphic design.

The X1 Carbon also supports multi-tasking with its powerful hardware and optimized software. Users can easily switch between open apps and windows using familiar gestures or keyboard shortcuts, maximizing productivity and workflow efficiency. The laptop's high-resolution display ensures crisp and clear visuals, making it easy to work on multiple tasks simultaneously without sacrificing clarity or performance.

In addition to navigating the Windows operating system, users can customize their X1 Carbon experience to suit their preferences and workflow requirements. Windows offers a wide range of customization options, including desktop backgrounds, themes, color schemes, and accessibility settings. Users can personalize their desktop environment to reflect their style and optimize their workflow for maximum efficiency.

For users who prefer alternative operating systems, the X1 Carbon offers compatibility with various Linux distributions, providing flexibility and choice in software options. Lenovo provides drivers and support for Linux-based systems, ensuring a smooth and seamless experience for users who prefer open-source software environments.

Overall, navigating the operating system on the Lenovo ThinkPad X1 Carbon (Gen 12, 2024) is a seamless and intuitive experience that empowers users to work, create, and collaborate with ease. Whether you're using Windows or another operating system, the X1 Carbon's powerful hardware, versatile input options, and customizable settings ensure a productive and enjoyable computing experience for users of all levels.

Customizing Settings for Optimal Performance

Customizing settings for optimal performance on the Lenovo ThinkPad X1 Carbon (Gen 12, 2024) is a crucial step in maximizing productivity, efficiency, and user experience. The X1 Carbon offers a range of customization options that allow users to tailor their laptop's settings to suit their preferences, workflow requirements, and performance needs.

One of the key areas for customization is power management. The X1 Carbon features advanced power settings that allow users to optimize battery life and performance based on their usage patterns. Users can choose from predefined power plans such as Balanced, Power Saver, and High Performance, or create custom power plans with specific settings for screen brightness, processor speed, and sleep modes. By adjusting these settings, users can extend battery life when on the go or boost performance for demanding tasks.

Another important aspect of customizing settings for optimal performance is managing system resources. The X1 Carbon comes equipped with powerful hardware components, including the latest Intel Core Ultra CPU, ample RAM, and fast SSD storage. Users can leverage these resources by adjusting system settings such as virtual memory, background apps, and startup programs to prioritize performance for specific tasks and applications. By fine-tuning these settings, users can ensure smooth multitasking, faster load times, and responsive performance across various workloads.

In addition to power management and resource allocation, users can customize display settings to enhance visual clarity and comfort. The X1 Carbon's high-resolution display offers crisp and vibrant visuals, but users can further optimize display settings such as brightness, color temperature, and screen scaling to reduce eye strain and improve readability. Customizing display settings not only enhances user comfort but also contributes to overall productivity and workflow efficiency.

The X1 Carbon also provides customization options for input devices such as the keyboard, touchpad, and pointing stick. Users can adjust keyboard shortcuts, key assignments, and touchpad sensitivity to match their typing style and navigation preferences. The inclusion of a TrackPoint pointing stick allows for precise cursor control, and users can customize TrackPoint settings such as pointer speed and scrolling behavior for optimal comfort and accuracy.

Furthermore, users can customize audio settings to enhance the audio experience on the X1 Carbon. The laptop features high-quality speakers and audio enhancements such as Dolby

Atmos support, allowing users to customize audio profiles, equalizer settings, and sound modes for immersive audio playback. Whether you're listening to music, watching videos, or participating in video conferences, customizing audio settings ensures a rich and enjoyable listening experience.

Security is another area where customization plays a crucial role on the X1 Carbon. Users can customize security settings such as biometric authentication, encryption options, and privacy controls to protect sensitive data and ensure a secure computing environment. By customizing security settings, users can mitigate risks, prevent unauthorized access, and safeguard their digital assets effectively.

Overall, customizing settings for optimal performance on the Lenovo ThinkPad X1 Carbon (Gen 12, 2024) empowers users to personalize their computing experience, improve productivity, and optimize the laptop's capabilities to meet their specific needs and preferences. By leveraging the range of customization options available, users can enhance performance, comfort, and security to create a seamless and efficient workflow.

Using the Keyboard, Touchpad, and TrackPoint

The Lenovo ThinkPad X1 Carbon (Gen 12, 2024) boasts a top-notch keyboard, a responsive touchpad, and the iconic TrackPoint, offering users a versatile and comfortable input experience. These input devices are meticulously designed to enhance productivity, accuracy, and user comfort, making them essential tools for navigating the laptop and interacting with applications and content.

The keyboard on the X1 Carbon is renowned for its exceptional quality and tactile feedback. The keys are well-spaced, with a comfortable key travel distance that strikes a balance between responsiveness and typing comfort. The keyboard layout follows the traditional ThinkPad design, featuring a full-size keyboard with dedicated function keys, arrow keys, and a numeric keypad (on select models). The keys are backlit, allowing for easy typing in low-light conditions and adding a touch of style to the laptop's aesthetic.

One of the standout features of the X1 Carbon's keyboard is its durability. The keys are constructed from high-quality materials, ensuring long-lasting performance even with heavy usage. The keyboard is spill-resistant, providing added protection against accidental spills and liquid damage. This durability makes the X1 Carbon's keyboard ideal for professionals who require a reliable and resilient input device for everyday use.

In addition to its durability, the X1 Carbon's keyboard offers a range of customization options to suit individual typing preferences. Users can adjust key sensitivity, key repeat rate, and keyboard backlighting settings through the laptop's settings menu, allowing for a personalized typing experience. The inclusion of multimedia keys and shortcut keys further enhances productivity, allowing users to perform common tasks and access frequently used functions with ease.

The touchpad on the X1 Carbon is equally impressive, offering precise cursor control and smooth navigation. The touchpad's surface is coated with a matte finish that provides a comfortable and responsive touch experience. Multi-touch gestures such as scrolling, zooming, and swiping are supported, allowing users to navigate through documents, web pages, and applications effortlessly. The touchpad's palm rejection technology ensures accurate input, even during multitasking or prolonged use.

Complementing the touchpad is Lenovo's iconic TrackPoint, also known as the pointing stick. The TrackPoint is a small, red pointing device located in the center of the keyboard, between the G, H, and B keys. It offers precise cursor control without the need to move your hands away from the keyboard, making it a favorite among users who prefer a more traditional input method. The TrackPoint's sensitivity and responsiveness can be customized through the laptop's settings, allowing users to fine-tune its behavior to their liking.

The combination of the keyboard, touchpad, and TrackPoint on the X1 Carbon provides users with a versatile and efficient input experience. Whether you're typing documents, navigating through spreadsheets, or browsing the web, these input devices ensure accuracy, comfort, and productivity. Their ergonomic design, customizable settings, and reliable performance make them essential components of the X1 Carbon's user experience, catering to the needs of professionals and power users alike.

Exploring Built-in Software and Applications

The Lenovo ThinkPad X1 Carbon (Gen 12, 2024) comes equipped with a range of built-in software and applications designed to enhance productivity, creativity, and convenience for users. These pre-installed software offerings provide users with essential tools and features out of the box, allowing them to get started with their work and tasks without the need for additional downloads or installations.

One of the key software offerings on the X1 Carbon is the Windows operating system, which provides a familiar and user-friendly interface for navigating the laptop and accessing various applications and settings. Windows offers a range of built-in apps such as Microsoft Edge for web browsing, Microsoft Office suite for productivity tasks, and Windows Media Player for multimedia playback. These apps are designed to work seamlessly with the X1

Carbon's hardware, providing a cohesive and integrated user experience.

In addition to Windows apps, Lenovo includes its own suite of software and utilities to enhance the functionality and performance of the X1 Carbon. One notable software is Lenovo Vantage, a comprehensive tool that allows users to manage system settings, update drivers, perform diagnostics, and customize device settings. Lenovo Vantage provides users with valuable insights into their laptop's health and performance, helping them optimize their experience and troubleshoot issues effectively.

Another built-in application on the X1 Carbon is Lenovo Intelligent Thermal Solution (ITS), which intelligently manages the laptop's thermal performance to ensure optimal cooling and efficiency. ITS adjusts fan speeds, power consumption, and thermal profiles based on workload and usage patterns, allowing users to maintain a comfortable and stable operating environment while maximizing performance.

For users who require security and privacy features, the X1 Carbon includes software such as Lenovo Privacy Manager and Lenovo Smart Assist. These applications provide users with tools to manage privacy settings, secure sensitive data, and protect against unauthorized access. Features such as facial recognition, fingerprint authentication, and encryption options enhance security and peace of mind for users.

Creative professionals will appreciate the inclusion of software such as Lenovo Pen Settings and Lenovo Quick Capture, which enhance the functionality of the optional stylus pen and built-in webcam, respectively. Lenovo Pen Settings allows users to customize pen sensitivity, button functions, and palm rejection settings for precise and intuitive input. Lenovo Quick Capture provides convenient access to the webcam for video calls, conferencing, and content creation.

In addition to productivity and security applications, the X1 Carbon includes entertainment and multimedia software to cater to a wide range of user preferences. Lenovo Entertainment Hub offers access to streaming services, digital content, and media libraries, allowing users to enjoy movies, music, and games on their laptop. Dolby Atmos support enhances the audio experience, delivering immersive sound quality for multimedia playback.

Overall, the built-in software and applications on the Lenovo ThinkPad X1 Carbon (Gen 12, 2024) provide users with a comprehensive and versatile computing experience. Whether you're a business professional, creative artist, or multimedia enthusiast, these pre-installed offerings offer valuable tools, features, and customization options to enhance productivity, creativity, and enjoyment on the X1 Carbon.

Chapter 3: Hardware Overview

The Lenovo ThinkPad X1 Carbon (Gen 12, 2024) is equipped with a range of high-performance hardware components that contribute to its exceptional functionality, reliability, and versatility. From the powerful processor to the advanced connectivity options, each hardware component is carefully selected and integrated to deliver a seamless computing experience for users in various industries and roles.

At the heart of the X1 Carbon is the Intel Core Ultra CPU, specifically the Ultra 7 155H chip running at 1.4 GHz. This cutting-edge processor provides a balance of power efficiency and performance, making it suitable for demanding tasks such as multitasking, content creation, and data processing. The Ultra CPU is designed to deliver improved artificial intelligence performance, better power efficiency, and enhanced integrated graphics capabilities, ensuring smooth and responsive performance across a wide range of applications.

Complementing the powerful processor is ample memory and storage capacity. The X1 Carbon is available with up to 32 GB of RAM, allowing users to run multiple applications simultaneously and switch between tasks with ease. The generous RAM capacity ensures smooth multitasking, fast data access, and responsive performance for intensive workloads. In terms of storage, the X1 Carbon offers up to a 1-TB solid-state drive (SSD), providing ample space for storing files, documents, media, and software. The SSD delivers fast read and write speeds, reducing loading times and improving overall system responsiveness.

The X1 Carbon's display is another standout feature, offering a stunning visual experience for work and entertainment. The laptop boasts a 14-inch LCD with a 16:10 aspect ratio and a resolution of 2880 x 1800 pixels. This high-resolution display delivers crisp and vibrant images with excellent color accuracy and sharpness, making it ideal for tasks such as content creation, graphic design, and multimedia editing. The wide viewing angles and anti-glare coating ensure comfortable viewing in various lighting conditions, while the touchscreen capabilities (optional) add a layer of interactivity and convenience for users.

Connectivity options on the X1 Carbon are robust and versatile, catering to modern workflow needs. The laptop features two Thunderbolt 4 USB-C ports, which support high-speed data transfer, power delivery, and external display connectivity. These ports are ideal for connecting peripherals, docking stations, and external displays, providing users with flexibility and convenience in expanding their workspace. Additionally, the X1 Carbon includes two USB-A ports for legacy devices, a full-size HDMI port for video output, and a SIM card slot (optional) for mobile connectivity.

Security features on the X1 Carbon are comprehensive and robust, ensuring data protection and privacy for users. The laptop includes a fingerprint reader for biometric authentication, allowing users to unlock the device securely and access sensitive data with ease. The webcam features a manual shutter for privacy, and Lenovo's security software suite provides encryption options, secure boot, and firmware protection to safeguard against cyber threats and unauthorized access.

In terms of audio and connectivity, the X1 Carbon excels with its high-quality speakers, Dolby Atmos support, and advanced wireless options. The laptop's audio system delivers crisp and immersive sound quality, enhancing the multimedia experience for users. Wireless connectivity options include Wi-Fi 6E for fast and reliable internet access, Bluetooth for wireless peripherals, and optional 5G connectivity for mobile broadband on the go.

The X1 Carbon's hardware components are meticulously designed and integrated to deliver a premium computing experience for professionals, creatives, and power users. Whether you're working on intensive tasks, collaborating with colleagues, or enjoying multimedia content, the X1 Carbon's powerful hardware ensures exceptional performance, reliability, and versatility to meet the demands of today's dynamic work environments.

Maintenance and Care Tips for the Hardware

Maintaining and caring for the hardware of your Lenovo ThinkPad X1 Carbon (Gen 12, 2024) is essential to ensure optimal performance, longevity, and reliability of your laptop. By following best practices and implementing regular maintenance routines, you can extend the lifespan of your hardware components and minimize the risk of potential issues or failures.

Here are some maintenance and care tips specifically tailored for the X1 Carbon's hardware:

1. Cleaning the exterior: Regularly clean the exterior of your X1 Carbon to remove dust, dirt, and debris that can accumulate over time. Use a soft, lint-free cloth slightly dampened with water or a mild cleaning solution to gently wipe down the laptop's surfaces, including the display, keyboard, touchpad, and casing. Avoid using harsh chemicals or abrasive materials that can damage the finish or components.

2. Keyboard and touchpad maintenance: Keep your keyboard and touchpad in good condition by cleaning them regularly. Use a can of compressed air to remove dust and particles from between the keys and around the touchpad. For stubborn dirt or debris, gently brush the keys and touchpad with a soft-bristled brush or cotton swab. Avoid spilling liquids or food particles on the keyboard and touchpad, and promptly clean up any spills to prevent damage.

3. Screen care: Protect the display of your X1 Carbon by avoiding direct contact with sharp or abrasive objects that can scratch or damage the screen. Use a microfiber cloth to gently clean the screen and remove fingerprints, smudges, and dust. Avoid using paper towels or rough materials that can scratch the display. Consider using a screen protector to add an extra layer of protection against scratches and minor impacts.

4. Battery maintenance: Properly maintain your X1 Carbon's battery to maximize its lifespan and performance. Avoid overcharging or fully discharging the battery frequently, as this can reduce its capacity over time. Use the laptop's power management settings to optimize battery usage and extend battery life. If possible, occasionally recalibrate the battery by fully charging and then fully discharging it to help maintain accurate battery capacity readings.

5. Ventilation and cooling: Ensure proper ventilation and cooling for your X1 Carbon to prevent overheating and thermal issues. Keep the laptop's air vents and fan intake areas free from obstructions such as dust, lint, or debris. Use the laptop on a flat, hard surface to allow for adequate airflow and cooling. Avoid using the laptop on soft surfaces such as beds or sofas that can block ventilation and cause overheating.

6. Hardware updates and maintenance: Regularly update your X1 Carbon's hardware drivers, firmware, and system software to ensure compatibility, performance improvements, and security enhancements. Use Lenovo's support website or Lenovo Vantage software to download and install updates for your laptop's hardware components. Additionally, periodically check for hardware issues or anomalies using diagnostic tools or built-in system diagnostics to detect and resolve potential problems early.

7. Physical protection: Protect your X1 Carbon from physical damage by using a laptop bag, sleeve, or case when transporting it. Avoid dropping or bumping the laptop, and handle it with care to prevent damage to fragile components such as the display, keyboard, and ports. Consider using a laptop lock or security cable to deter theft and secure your laptop in public or shared environments.

By following these maintenance and care tips for your Lenovo ThinkPad X1 Carbon (Gen 12, 2024), you can ensure the longevity, reliability, and optimal performance of your laptop's hardware components. Regular cleaning, proper battery management, ventilation maintenance, software updates, and physical protection are key aspects of maintaining a healthy and well-functioning laptop that meets your computing needs for years to come.

Tips for Improving Battery Life

Improving battery life on your Lenovo ThinkPad X1 Carbon (Gen 12, 2024) is essential for maximizing productivity, mobility, and convenience. By implementing effective battery-saving techniques and optimizing power settings, you can extend the battery life of your laptop and enjoy longer usage times between charges. Here are some tips for improving battery life on your X1 Carbon:

1. Adjust power settings: Optimize your X1 Carbon's power settings to balance performance and battery life. Use the Power Options or Battery settings in Windows to select a power plan that suits your usage needs. Choose a Balanced or Power Saver plan to reduce energy consumption and extend battery life. Customize advanced settings such as screen brightness, sleep mode, and processor performance to further conserve power.

2. Manage background apps: Close or disable unnecessary background apps and processes that consume system resources and drain the battery. Use Task Manager or system settings to identify and terminate resource-intensive apps, browser tabs, and startup programs. Limiting background activity helps reduce CPU usage, RAM usage, and power consumption, leading to improved battery life.

3. Reduce screen brightness: Lower the screen brightness of your X1 Carbon to conserve battery power. Adjust the display brightness manually or enable adaptive brightness settings to automatically adjust brightness based on ambient light conditions. Dimming the screen reduces energy consumption significantly, especially when working in well-lit environments or using the laptop for extended periods.

4. Enable battery saver mode: Activate the battery saver mode on your X1 Carbon to automatically adjust system settings and optimize power usage. Battery saver mode conserves energy by reducing background activity, disabling non-essential features, and adjusting system performance for efficiency. Customize battery saver settings to specify actions such as dimming the display, limiting background apps, and adjusting power profiles.

5. Disconnect peripherals: Unplug or disconnect external peripherals and devices such as USB drives, external hard drives, printers, and accessories when not in use. Connected peripherals consume additional power and can drain the battery faster, especially if they require constant data transfer or charging. Disconnecting unused peripherals helps conserve battery life and reduces power consumption.

6. Use battery optimization tools: Take advantage of battery optimization tools and utilities provided by Lenovo or third-party software to monitor, manage, and optimize battery usage. Lenovo Vantage software offers features such as Battery Stretch, Battery Charge Threshold, and Battery Gauge to enhance battery performance, longevity, and health. Use these tools to customize charging settings, calibrate the battery, and track battery usage over time.

7. Avoid extreme temperatures: Protect your X1 Carbon's battery from exposure to extreme temperatures, as high heat or cold can negatively impact battery life and performance. Keep the laptop in a well-ventilated area with moderate temperatures to prevent overheating or excessive cooling. Avoid leaving the laptop in direct sunlight, near heating vents, or in hot/cold environments for prolonged periods.

8. Update firmware and drivers: Regularly update your X1 Carbon's firmware, drivers, and system software to ensure compatibility, performance improvements, and battery optimization. Use Lenovo's support website or Lenovo Vantage software to download and install updates for your laptop's hardware components. Updated firmware and drivers often include enhancements that improve battery efficiency, power management, and overall system stability.

9. Use battery maintenance features: Take advantage of built-in battery maintenance features and options to extend battery life and maintain optimal performance. Enable features such as Battery Charge Threshold, which limits the maximum battery charge level to reduce wear and prolong battery lifespan. Use Battery Gauge to monitor battery health, capacity, and charging patterns for proactive maintenance and optimization.

By implementing these tips for improving battery life on your Lenovo ThinkPad X1 Carbon (Gen 12, 2024), you can maximize the usability, efficiency, and longevity of your laptop's battery. Conserving power, optimizing settings, managing background activity, and maintaining proper battery care habits contribute to an enhanced computing experience with extended battery runtime for your everyday tasks and activities.

Optimizing Storage and Memory Usage

Optimizing storage and memory usage on your Lenovo ThinkPad X1 Carbon (Gen 12, 2024) is crucial for ensuring efficient performance, fast access to data, and seamless multitasking. By implementing storage management techniques and memory optimization strategies, you can maximize the available resources on your laptop and improve overall system responsiveness. Here are some tips for optimizing storage and memory usage on your X1 Carbon:

1. Organize and declutter storage: Start by organizing and decluttering your storage space to free up valuable disk space and improve system performance. Remove unnecessary files, temporary data, and old applications that are no longer in use. Use built-in disk cleanup tools or third-party software to identify and delete junk files, cache data, and redundant files that consume storage space.

2. Use storage optimization tools: Take advantage of storage optimization tools and utilities to manage and optimize your X1 Carbon's storage space effectively. Use disk defragmentation tools to consolidate fragmented files and improve disk read/write speeds.

Consider using disk cleanup tools that analyze disk usage, identify large files or folders, and provide recommendations for freeing up space.

3. Utilize cloud storage: Offload large files, media libraries, and infrequently accessed data to cloud storage solutions such as Google Drive, Microsoft OneDrive, or Dropbox. Cloud storage offers scalable storage options, data synchronization across devices, and convenient access to files from anywhere with an internet connection. Use cloud storage for backing up important files, reducing local storage usage, and optimizing disk space on your X1 Carbon.

4. Manage virtual memory: Optimize virtual memory settings to improve system performance and responsiveness. Adjust the virtual memory (page file) size based on your usage patterns and available RAM. Increase the virtual memory size if you frequently run memory-intensive applications or multitask heavily. Ensure that the virtual memory settings are properly configured to prevent excessive disk swapping and performance degradation.

5. Monitor memory usage: Monitor and manage memory usage on your X1 Carbon to identify and address memory-related issues. Use Task Manager or system monitoring tools to track memory usage, identify memory-hungry applications, and detect memory leaks or excessive resource consumption. Close unused or idle applications, browser tabs, and background processes to free up memory and improve system responsiveness.

6. Optimize startup programs: Review and optimize startup programs to reduce system boot time and improve overall performance. Disable unnecessary startup programs and background services that launch automatically with Windows. Use Task Manager or system settings to manage startup programs, prioritize essential applications, and reduce system resource overhead during startup.

7. Upgrade hardware components: Consider upgrading hardware components such as RAM and storage to improve performance and expand capacity. Upgrade to a higher-capacity SSD for faster data access and storage space. Increase RAM capacity to accommodate multitasking, intensive applications, and future software requirements. Upgrading hardware components can significantly enhance system performance and responsiveness for demanding tasks.

8. Use memory optimization software: Install and use memory optimization software or utilities to manage and optimize RAM usage on your X1 Carbon. Memory optimization tools can help identify memory leaks, optimize memory allocation, and improve system stability. Consider using tools that offer real-time monitoring, automatic memory management, and customizable settings for optimizing memory usage.

By implementing these tips for optimizing storage and memory usage on your Lenovo

ThinkPad X1 Carbon (Gen 12, 2024), you can enhance system performance, responsiveness, and efficiency. Conserving storage space, managing memory usage, optimizing virtual memory settings, and upgrading hardware components contribute to a smoother computing experience with improved multitasking capabilities and faster access to data and applications.

Chapter 4: Connectivity and Networking

Connecting to Wi-Fi Networks

Connecting to Wi-Fi networks on your Lenovo ThinkPad X1 Carbon (Gen 12, 2024) is a straightforward process that allows you to access the internet, share files, and communicate wirelessly. Whether you're at home, in the office, or on the go, connecting to Wi-Fi networks provides you with the flexibility and convenience of wireless connectivity. Here's a guide on how to connect to Wi-Fi networks on your X1 Carbon:

1. Enable Wi-Fi: Start by ensuring that the Wi-Fi feature on your X1 Carbon is enabled. Locate the Wi-Fi icon in the system tray on the taskbar, usually represented by a series of bars or waves. If the Wi-Fi icon is grayed out or disabled, right-click on it and select "Enable Wi-Fi" or a similar option to activate the Wi-Fi adapter.

2. Scan for available networks: Once Wi-Fi is enabled, click on the Wi-Fi icon in the system tray to open the list of available Wi-Fi networks. Your X1 Carbon will scan for nearby Wi-Fi networks and display a list of detected networks. Wait for the scanning process to complete, and the list of available networks will appear in the Wi-Fi menu.

3. Select the desired network: From the list of available networks, locate and select the Wi-Fi network you want to connect to. The network names (SSIDs) will be displayed along with their signal strength and security status. Choose the network you want to join by clicking on it or selecting it from the list.

4. Enter network credentials: If the selected Wi-Fi network is secured (encrypted), you will be prompted to enter the network password or security key. Type the Wi-Fi password correctly to ensure a successful connection. If you're connecting to a public or guest network that doesn't require a password, you may be automatically connected without entering any credentials.

5. Connect to the network: After entering the correct network credentials, click on the "Connect" or "Join" button to initiate the connection process. Your X1 Carbon will attempt to establish a connection to the selected Wi-Fi network using the provided credentials. A status message will indicate whether the connection was successful or if there are any issues.

6. Wait for connection confirmation: Once the connection process is initiated, wait for a few moments for your X1 Carbon to establish a connection to the Wi-Fi network. You may see a spinning icon or progress indicator while the connection is being established. Once connected, the Wi-Fi icon in the system tray will change to indicate a successful connection, and you will have internet access.

7. Troubleshoot connection issues: If you encounter any difficulties or errors during the connection process, troubleshoot the issue by checking the network credentials, signal strength, and Wi-Fi adapter settings. Ensure that the Wi-Fi signal is strong and stable, and that the network password is entered correctly. You can also troubleshoot Wi-Fi connectivity issues using Windows Network Troubleshooter or Lenovo Vantage's network diagnostics tools.

8. Manage saved networks: Your X1 Carbon can save and remember Wi-Fi networks that you've connected to in the past. You can manage saved networks, prioritize preferred networks, and forget unwanted networks using the Wi-Fi settings in Windows or Lenovo Vantage. This allows you to easily reconnect to known networks and manage your Wi-Fi connections efficiently.

By following these steps and guidelines, you can successfully connect to Wi-Fi networks on your Lenovo ThinkPad X1 Carbon (Gen 12, 2024) and enjoy wireless internet connectivity for your work, communication, and entertainment needs.

Using Bluetooth and other Wireless Technologies

Using Bluetooth and other wireless technologies on your Lenovo ThinkPad X1 Carbon (Gen 12, 2024) expands connectivity options, allowing you to wirelessly connect to peripherals, devices, and accessories. Bluetooth technology enables seamless communication and data transfer between your laptop and compatible devices, while other wireless technologies such as NFC (Near Field Communication) and Wi-Fi Direct offer additional functionalities. Here's a comprehensive guide on how to use Bluetooth and other wireless technologies on your X1 Carbon:

1. Bluetooth connectivity: Enable Bluetooth on your X1 Carbon to start pairing and connecting to Bluetooth-enabled devices. Open the Windows Settings app and navigate to the "Devices" section. Select "Bluetooth & other devices" and toggle the Bluetooth switch to turn it on. Your X1 Carbon will start scanning for nearby Bluetooth devices.

2. Pairing Bluetooth devices: To pair a Bluetooth device such as a wireless keyboard, mouse, headset, or speaker, ensure that the device is in pairing mode. In the Bluetooth settings on your X1 Carbon, click on "Add Bluetooth or other device" and select the device type you want to add. Follow the on-screen instructions to complete the pairing process, which may involve entering a pairing code or confirming the connection on both devices.

3. Managing Bluetooth devices: Once paired, manage your Bluetooth devices in the Bluetooth settings menu. You can rename devices for easy identification, remove or forget devices you no longer use, and adjust device settings such as audio profiles for headphones or speaker systems. Manage Bluetooth devices efficiently to streamline connectivity and optimize performance.

4. Using Bluetooth for file transfer: Bluetooth can also be used for file transfer between your X1 Carbon and other Bluetooth-enabled devices. Use the Bluetooth File Transfer feature to send and receive files, photos, videos, and documents wirelessly. Select the file you want to share, right-click, and choose the "Send to" or "Share" option, then select the Bluetooth device as the destination.

5. NFC (Near Field Communication): If your X1 Carbon supports NFC technology, you can use it for quick and easy pairing with NFC-enabled devices. NFC allows for seamless communication and data exchange by simply bringing devices close together. Enable NFC in your laptop's settings and follow the device-specific instructions for NFC pairing and connectivity.

6. Wi-Fi Direct: Wi-Fi Direct enables direct wireless communication between your X1 Carbon and other Wi-Fi Direct-compatible devices without the need for a traditional Wi-Fi network. Use Wi-Fi Direct to share files, stream media, and collaborate with compatible devices such as smartphones, tablets, and printers. Enable Wi-Fi Direct in your laptop's settings and follow device-specific instructions for establishing a Wi-Fi Direct connection.

7. Using wireless displays: Connect your X1 Carbon to wireless displays and projectors using Miracast or other wireless display technologies. Enable wireless display settings on your laptop and select the target display device from the list of available wireless displays. Follow the on-screen instructions to establish a wireless display connection and mirror or extend your laptop's screen wirelessly.

8. Bluetooth and wireless accessories: Explore a wide range of Bluetooth and wireless accessories that enhance productivity and convenience on your X1 Carbon. Consider using Bluetooth keyboards, mice, headsets, and speakers for wireless input, audio, and communication. Connect wirelessly to printers, scanners, external displays, and smart home devices for seamless integration and functionality.

By leveraging Bluetooth and other wireless technologies on your Lenovo ThinkPad X1 Carbon (Gen 12, 2024), you can enhance connectivity, productivity, and versatility for various tasks and applications. From pairing Bluetooth devices and transferring files to using NFC, Wi-Fi Direct, and wireless displays, your X1 Carbon offers a range of wireless capabilities that streamline workflows and enhance your computing experience.

Configuring Network Settings for Business and Personal Use

Configuring network settings on your Lenovo ThinkPad X1 Carbon (Gen 12, 2024) for both business and personal use is essential for establishing reliable and secure network connections. Whether you're connecting to corporate networks, home networks, or public Wi-Fi hotspots, configuring network settings ensures seamless connectivity, optimal performance, and protection against security threats. Here's a detailed guide on how to configure network settings for business and personal use on your X1 Carbon:

1. Network connection types: Understand the different types of network connections available on your X1 Carbon, including wired Ethernet, Wi-Fi, and cellular data (if applicable). Determine which network connection type is suitable for your current environment and usage requirements. For business use, prioritize secure and stable network connections, while for personal use, consider convenience and flexibility.

2. Wired Ethernet configuration: If you're connecting to a wired Ethernet network in a business environment, configure Ethernet settings on your X1 Carbon for reliable and high-speed connectivity. Connect an Ethernet cable to the laptop's Ethernet port and access the Network settings in Windows. Configure Ethernet adapter settings such as IP address, subnet mask, gateway, and DNS server addresses based on network requirements or

DHCP (Dynamic Host Configuration Protocol) settings.

3. Wi-Fi network configuration: For wireless Wi-Fi network connections, configure Wi-Fi settings on your X1 Carbon to connect to home networks, office networks, or public Wi-Fi hotspots securely. Open the Wi-Fi settings in Windows and select the desired Wi-Fi network from the available networks list. Enter the Wi-Fi password (if required) and configure advanced settings such as Wi-Fi security protocols (WPA2, WPA3), SSID visibility, and network profiles for automatic connection.

4. VPN (Virtual Private Network) setup: For secure remote access to business networks and data, set up a VPN connection on your X1 Carbon. Configure VPN settings in Windows by adding a new VPN connection and entering the VPN server address, authentication credentials, VPN protocol (IKEv2, L2TP/IPsec, SSTP), and other connection details provided by your IT department or VPN service provider. Enable

VPN auto-connect or on-demand connection options for seamless VPN connectivity.

5. Proxy server configuration: In business environments with proxy servers, configure proxy settings on your X1 Carbon to route network traffic through the proxy server for web browsing, network access, and security compliance. Access proxy settings in Windows and enter the proxy server address, port number, authentication credentials (if required), and proxy bypass rules as per organizational policies and network configuration.

6. Network sharing and permissions: Configure network sharing settings on your X1 Carbon for sharing files, printers, and resources with other devices on the network. Enable file and printer sharing options in Windows, set up shared folders or drives, and define permissions for access control (read-only, read/write) based on user accounts or network groups. Ensure that network discovery and file sharing protocols

(SMB, NFS) are enabled for seamless network collaboration.

7. Firewall and network security: Enable and configure Windows Firewall settings on your X1 Carbon to protect against unauthorized network access, malicious traffic, and cyber threats. Customize firewall rules, inbound/outbound port settings, application permissions, and network profiles (private, public, domain) to enhance network security without compromising usability. Consider using third-party firewall solutions for advanced network protection and intrusion prevention.

8. Network troubleshooting and diagnostics: Familiarize yourself with network troubleshooting tools and diagnostics utilities on your X1 Carbon to troubleshoot connectivity issues, network errors, and performance problems. Use built-in Windows Network Troubleshooter, Command Prompt tools (ping, ipconfig), Network and Sharing Center, and Lenovo Vantage network diagnostics for identifying and resolving network issues effectively.

By following these steps and guidelines for configuring network settings on your Lenovo ThinkPad X1 Carbon (Gen 12, 2024), you can establish reliable, secure, and optimized network connections for both business and personal use. Ensure proper network configuration, security protocols, VPN setup, and network sharing settings to enhance productivity, collaboration, and connectivity across various network environments and scenarios.

Chapter 5: Security Features

The Lenovo ThinkPad X1 Carbon (Gen 12, 2024) offers robust security features and advanced biometric options to ensure data protection, privacy, and access control. These security measures are designed to safeguard sensitive information, prevent unauthorized access, and enhance overall security posture. Let's explore an overview of the security features and biometric options available on the X1 Carbon:

1. Fingerprint Reader: The X1 Carbon is equipped with a fingerprint reader that allows users to log in to their laptops securely using biometric authentication. The fingerprint reader is integrated into the laptop's keyboard or touchpad, providing a convenient and reliable way to verify user identity. Users can enroll their fingerprints in the system and use them as a biometric credential for unlocking the device, accessing files, and authenticating transactions.

2. Windows Hello Facial Recognition: For enhanced biometric security, the X1 Carbon supports Windows Hello facial recognition technology. This feature enables users to log in to their laptops by scanning their faces using the built-in webcam. Windows Hello facial recognition uses advanced algorithms to create a unique facial profile, ensuring accurate and secure authentication without the need for passwords or PINs. Users can configure Windows Hello facial recognition in Windows settings and enjoy seamless and secure access to their devices.

3. Hardware-based Security Chip: The X1 Carbon incorporates a hardware-based security chip, such as the Trusted Platform Module (TPM), to provide hardware-level security functionalities. The TPM securely stores encryption keys, digital certificates, and sensitive data, protecting them from unauthorized access and tampering. It enables secure boot processes, data encryption, and authentication protocols, contributing to a secure computing environment.

4. BIOS/UEFI Security: The X1 Carbon includes BIOS (Basic Input/Output System) or UEFI (Unified Extensible Firmware Interface) security features to protect the system firmware from unauthorized modifications and malware attacks. Secure Boot, Secure BIOS Update, and

BIOS password protection are some of the BIOS/UEFI security mechanisms implemented on the X1 Carbon. These features help ensure the integrity and authenticity of the system firmware, mitigating potential security risks.

5. Encryption and Data Protection: To safeguard sensitive data, the X1 Carbon supports encryption technologies such as BitLocker (for Windows) or FileVault (for macOS). These encryption solutions encrypt data stored on the laptop's disk drives, protecting it from unauthorized access in case of theft or loss. Users can enable encryption and manage encryption keys to ensure data confidentiality and compliance with security standards.

6. Virtual Private Network (VPN) Support: The X1 Carbon facilitates secure remote access to corporate networks and resources through VPN connectivity. Users can configure VPN connections using built-in VPN clients or third-party VPN software to establish encrypted tunnels and protect data transmission over untrusted networks. VPN support enhances privacy, confidentiality, and network security for remote workers and mobile users.

7. Antivirus and Security Software: Lenovo collaborates with leading cybersecurity vendors to provide pre-installed antivirus and security software on the X1 Carbon. These security solutions offer real-time threat detection, malware protection, firewall capabilities, and secure web browsing features. Users can activate and configure security software to defend against cyber threats, phishing attacks, and malicious activities.

8. Privacy Features: The X1 Carbon incorporates privacy features such as physical camera shutters (ThinkShutter) and microphone mute buttons to enhance privacy protection. ThinkShutter allows users to physically cover the webcam when not in use, preventing unauthorized camera access and ensuring privacy during video calls or conferences. The microphone mute button disables the microphone to prevent eavesdropping and unauthorized audio recording.

The Lenovo ThinkPad X1 Carbon (Gen 12, 2024) offers a comprehensive suite of security features and advanced biometric options to meet the stringent security requirements of modern computing environments. From fingerprint readers and facial recognition to hardware-based security, encryption, VPN support, and privacy features, the X1 Carbon prioritizes security and privacy without compromising usability and productivity. Users can leverage these security capabilities to protect their data, identities, and devices against cybersecurity threats and vulnerabilities, ensuring a secure and trusted computing experience.

Setting Up Passwords and Encryption

Setting up passwords and encryption on your Lenovo ThinkPad X1 Carbon (Gen 12, 2024) is crucial for securing sensitive data, protecting privacy, and preventing unauthorized access to your device and files. Passwords and encryption serve as fundamental security measures that help mitigate risks and ensure data confidentiality. Here's a comprehensive guide on how to set up passwords and encryption on your X1 Carbon:

1. Password Creation Guidelines: When setting up passwords on your X1 Carbon, follow best practices to create strong and secure passwords. Consider the following guidelines:

- Use a combination of uppercase and lowercase letters, numbers, and special characters.
- Avoid using easily guessable information such as birthdays, names, or common words.
- Aim for a password length of at least 12 characters to enhance complexity and resilience against brute-force attacks.
- Use unique passwords for different accounts and avoid reusing passwords across multiple platforms.

2. Setting a BIOS Password: Start by setting a BIOS (Basic Input/Output System) password on your X1 Carbon to protect the system firmware and BIOS settings from unauthorized modifications. Access the BIOS setup utility by restarting your laptop and pressing the appropriate key (often F1, F2, or Del) during the boot process to enter BIOS settings. Navigate to the Security or BIOS Security section and set a strong BIOS password. This password prevents unauthorized users from accessing or tampering with BIOS configurations.

3. Windows User Account Password: Ensure that your Windows user account is protected by a strong password. Open the Windows Settings app, go to Accounts > Sign-in options, and select "Password" under the "Password, PIN, or Windows Hello" section. Create or change your Windows password following the password creation guidelines mentioned earlier. You can also enable additional security features such as Windows Hello facial recognition or fingerprint login for biometric authentication.

4. File and Folder Encryption: Use built-in encryption tools such as BitLocker (for Windows) or FileVault (for macOS) to encrypt sensitive files and folders on your X1 Carbon's disk drives. Encrypting files and folders adds an extra layer of security, ensuring that even if someone gains unauthorized access to your device, they cannot access the encrypted data without the encryption key. Right-click on a file or folder, select "Properties," and enable encryption options to encrypt selected items.

5. Full Disk Encryption: Consider enabling full disk encryption (FDE) using BitLocker Drive Encryption (Windows) or FileVault (macOS) to encrypt the entire contents of your X1 Carbon's disk drives. Full disk encryption protects all data stored on the disk, including system files, applications, and user data. Enable BitLocker or FileVault encryption in the Windows Security Center or macOS System Preferences, respectively, and follow the on-screen instructions to encrypt your disk drives.

6. Secure Boot and Device Encryption: Ensure that Secure Boot is enabled in the BIOS settings to prevent unauthorized boot loaders or operating systems from running during the boot process. Secure Boot enhances system security by verifying the integrity and authenticity of boot components. Additionally, enable device encryption features such as Windows Device Encryption (for Windows 10 Pro and Enterprise editions) for added data protection and security.

7. Password Manager Usage: Consider using a reputable password manager application to store and manage your passwords securely. Password managers encrypt and store passwords in a secure vault, allowing you to access them with a master password or biometric authentication. Password managers also generate strong passwords, autofill login credentials, and sync passwords across devices for convenience and security.

8. Regular Password Updates: Periodically update your passwords and encryption keys to maintain security and prevent potential vulnerabilities. Change passwords at least every three to six months or immediately after any security incident or suspected compromise. Use unique and complex passwords for different accounts and devices to minimize security risks.

By following these steps and implementing strong passwords, encryption protocols, and security practices on your Lenovo ThinkPad X1 Carbon (Gen 12, 2024), you can enhance data protection, mitigate security threats, and safeguard your device and personal information effectively. Passwords and encryption play a critical role in maintaining a secure computing environment and ensuring peace of mind regarding data security and privacy.

Best Practices for Securing Your Data and Privacy

Securing your data and privacy on your Lenovo ThinkPad X1 Carbon (Gen 12, 2024) involves implementing best practices that protect sensitive information, prevent unauthorized access, and minimize security risks. By following these best practices, you can enhance data security, safeguard your privacy, and maintain a secure computing environment. Here are the key best practices for securing your data and privacy on the X1 Carbon:

1. Use Strong and Unique Passwords: Create strong and complex passwords for your user accounts, BIOS settings, and encryption keys. Avoid using easily guessable passwords and consider using a password manager to generate and store strong passwords securely. Use different passwords for different accounts and change passwords regularly to reduce the risk of password compromise.

2. Enable Multi-Factor Authentication (MFA): Implement multi-factor authentication (MFA) wherever possible to add an extra layer of security to your accounts. MFA requires users to provide multiple forms of verification, such as a password and a one-time code sent to a mobile device, to access accounts. Enable MFA for online services, email accounts, and critical applications to enhance authentication security.

3. Keep Software and Firmware Updated: Regularly update your operating system, applications, device drivers, and firmware to patch security vulnerabilities and ensure that you have the latest security patches and bug fixes. Enable automatic updates whenever possible to receive timely security updates and protect against known exploits and vulnerabilities.

4. Enable Firewall and Antivirus Protection: Activate Windows Firewall or use third-party firewall solutions to monitor and block unauthorized network traffic and incoming threats. Install reputable antivirus and anti-malware software on your X1 Carbon to detect and remove malicious software, viruses, and malware that may compromise your data and privacy.

5. Encrypt Sensitive Data: Use encryption technologies such as BitLocker (for Windows) or FileVault (for macOS) to encrypt sensitive data stored on your X1 Carbon's disk drives. Encrypt files, folders, and entire disk volumes to protect data confidentiality and prevent unauthorized access in case of theft or loss. Enable encryption features in the operating system settings and manage encryption keys securely.

6. Secure Wireless Networks: When connecting to Wi-Fi networks, use secure and encrypted Wi-Fi protocols (WPA2, WPA3) to prevent eavesdropping and unauthorized access. Avoid connecting to unsecured public Wi-Fi networks, and use a virtual private network (VPN) for secure and encrypted internet connections, especially when accessing sensitive information or conducting online transactions.

7. Backup Data Regularly: Implement a regular backup strategy to create copies of important data and files stored on your X1 Carbon. Use cloud backup services, external hard drives, or network-attached storage (NAS) devices to store backups securely. Regular backups protect against data loss due to hardware failure, theft, malware, or accidental deletion.

8. Secure Physical Access: Protect your X1 Carbon from unauthorized physical access by using security features such as BIOS passwords, fingerprint readers, and physical camera shutters (ThinkShutter). Keep your laptop physically secure and avoid leaving it unattended in public places where it may be vulnerable to theft or tampering.

9. Educate and Train Users: Educate yourself and other users (such as family members or colleagues) about cybersecurity best practices, phishing awareness, and social engineering threats. Train users to recognize suspicious emails, links, and attachments, and encourage them to report security incidents or unusual activities promptly.

10. Monitor and Audit Security: Regularly monitor and audit your X1 Carbon's security settings, event logs, and system activity for signs of potential security breaches or anomalies. Use security monitoring tools, intrusion detection systems (IDS), and security information and event management (SIEM) solutions to detect and respond to security incidents proactively.

By implementing these best practices for securing your data and privacy on your Lenovo ThinkPad X1 Carbon (Gen 12, 2024), you can mitigate security risks, protect sensitive information, and maintain a resilient cybersecurity posture. Stay vigilant, update security measures regularly, and adopt a proactive approach to data security to safeguard your digital assets and privacy effectively.

Chapter 6: Troubleshooting and Support

Common Issues and Troubleshooting Steps

When using your Lenovo ThinkPad X1 Carbon (Gen 12, 2024), you may encounter common issues that can affect performance, connectivity, and overall user experience. Knowing how to troubleshoot these issues effectively can help resolve problems and ensure smooth operation. Here are some common issues and troubleshooting steps for the X1 Carbon:

1. Slow Performance

- Check for background processes and applications consuming excessive CPU or memory resources. Close unnecessary programs and tabs to free up system resources.

- Update device drivers, BIOS, and firmware to the latest versions to improve compatibility and performance.
- Run a disk cleanup and defragmentation to optimize disk space and improve disk performance.
- Disable startup programs and services that may be slowing down the system boot process.
- Consider upgrading hardware components such as RAM or SSD for enhanced performance, if feasible.

2. Wi-Fi Connectivity Issues

- Ensure that Wi-Fi is enabled on your X1 Carbon and that the correct network SSID (Wi-Fi name) is selected.
- Check Wi-Fi signal strength and proximity to the wireless router or access

point. Move closer to the router for better signal reception.

- Restart the Wi-Fi router or access point to reset network settings and resolve temporary connectivity issues.

- Update Wi-Fi drivers and firmware on your X1 Carbon to the latest versions for improved compatibility and performance.

- Disable and re-enable Wi-Fi, or use the Windows Network Troubleshooter to diagnose and fix Wi-Fi connectivity problems.

3. Battery Drain or Charging Issues

- Check the battery status and power settings on your X1 Carbon. Adjust power settings to optimize battery life and reduce power consumption.

- Verify that the power adapter is properly connected to the laptop and power outlet. Inspect the power cable for any damage or wear.

- Clean the charging port and connectors on both the laptop and power adapter to ensure a secure connection.
- Update battery drivers and firmware, if available, to address compatibility issues and improve battery performance.
- If the battery does not charge or drains quickly, consider replacing the battery or contacting Lenovo support for further assistance.

4. Display or Graphics Problems

- Adjust display settings such as resolution, brightness, and refresh rate to optimize visual quality and reduce strain on the eyes.
- Update graphics drivers to the latest versions to ensure compatibility with graphics-intensive applications and games.
- Check for loose or damaged display cables and connectors. Reconnect or replace cables as needed.

- Run diagnostic tests for display hardware and graphics performance using built-in Lenovo diagnostics or third-party software tools.
- If the display shows artifacts, flickering, or distorted images, contact Lenovo support for potential display hardware replacement or repair.

5. Software Compatibility Issues

- Ensure that software applications and drivers are compatible with your X1 Carbon and the installed operating system (Windows or macOS).
- Update software applications, drivers, and firmware to the latest versions to address compatibility issues and improve performance.
- Check for software updates and patches from application developers or Lenovo's support website.
- If a specific software application crashes or behaves unexpectedly, try reinstalling

the application or using compatibility mode settings.

6. BIOS or System Configuration Errors

- Verify that BIOS settings are configured correctly and match recommended settings for optimal system performance.
- Reset BIOS settings to default values if you suspect configuration errors or instability issues.
- Update BIOS firmware to the latest version to address known bugs, compatibility issues, and security vulnerabilities.
- Use BIOS diagnostics tools or Lenovo Vantage software to diagnose and troubleshoot hardware-related problems at the BIOS level.

7. Peripheral Device Connectivity Problems

- Ensure that peripheral devices such as USB drives, printers, and external monitors are connected securely to the appropriate ports on your X1 Carbon.

- Install device drivers and software for peripherals to enable proper functionality and compatibility with your laptop.
- Check for loose or damaged cables, connectors, or ports on both the laptop and peripheral devices. Replace faulty cables or connectors as needed.
- Use Windows Device Manager or Lenovo Vantage to diagnose and troubleshoot device connectivity issues, such as unrecognized devices or driver conflicts.

8. Overheating or Fan Noise

- Clean the laptop's air vents and cooling system regularly to remove dust and debris that can obstruct airflow and cause overheating.
- Place your X1 Carbon on a flat, hard surface to ensure adequate ventilation and cooling.

- Adjust power settings to optimize performance and reduce heat generation, especially during intensive tasks or gaming.
- Update BIOS and thermal management drivers to improve fan control and thermal performance.
- If overheating persists, consider using a laptop cooling pad or contacting Lenovo support for further assistance.

By following these troubleshooting steps and addressing common issues effectively, you can maintain optimal performance, connectivity, and reliability for your Lenovo ThinkPad X1 Carbon (Gen 12, 2024). If problems persist or if you encounter hardware-related issues, contact Lenovo support or consult a professional technician for assistance.

Chapter 7: Advanced Tips and Tricks

Advanced Customization Options

Advanced customization options on the Lenovo ThinkPad X1 Carbon (Gen 12, 2024) allow users to tailor their computing experience, optimize productivity, and personalize the laptop according to their preferences and workflow. From system settings to hardware configurations, the X1 Carbon offers a range of advanced customization features that enhance usability, performance, and user satisfaction. Here are some key areas of advanced customization on the X1 Carbon:

1. Power Management and Performance Settings.

- Customize power management settings to balance performance and battery life. Adjust power plans in Windows settings or Lenovo Vantage software to optimize CPU performance, screen brightness, sleep modes, and power-saving features.

- Fine-tune performance profiles for specific tasks such as gaming, video editing, or productivity. Use Lenovo Vantage's Intelligent Cooling mode to dynamically adjust fan speed and thermal management based on workload.

2. Keyboard Customization and Hotkeys

- Customize keyboard shortcuts and function keys to launch applications, perform system tasks, or control multimedia functions. Use Lenovo Vantage or keyboard customization software to assign custom hotkeys and macros for efficient workflow navigation.
- Configure keyboard backlight settings, including brightness levels and automatic backlight adjustment based on ambient light conditions. Customize key

illumination patterns and colors for visual aesthetics and usability.

3. Touchpad and TrackPoint Settings

- Adjust touchpad sensitivity, scrolling speed, and gesture controls to suit your preferences. Customize tap-to-click, two-finger scrolling, pinch-to-zoom, and other touchpad gestures for intuitive navigation.
- Customize TrackPoint sensitivity, acceleration, and button configurations for precise cursor control and ergonomic usage. Enable or disable TrackPoint features such as scrolling, magnifying, or launching applications with TrackPoint buttons.

4. Display and Graphics Customization

- Customize display settings such as resolution, refresh rate, color calibration, and external monitor configurations. Use

Windows display settings or graphics control panels (Intel Graphics Command Center, NVIDIA Control Panel) to adjust display properties and optimize visual quality.

- Enable or disable advanced display features such as HDR (High Dynamic Range), adaptive sync, or color profiles for accurate color reproduction and immersive viewing experiences.

5. Sound and Audio Settings

- Customize audio output settings, equalizer presets, and volume levels for built-in speakers, headphones, or external audio devices. Use audio control panels or software applications to adjust sound profiles, enhance bass, or enable virtual surround sound.
- Configure microphone settings, noise cancellation, and recording levels for clear voice communication and multimedia recording. Adjust microphone sensitivity

and audio input sources for optimal performance during video calls or content creation.

6. Security and Privacy Options

- Customize security settings such as biometric authentication (fingerprint, facial recognition), encryption protocols (BitLocker, FileVault), and secure boot configurations. Use Windows Security Center, Lenovo Vantage Security features, or BIOS settings to manage security options and protect sensitive data.
- Enable privacy features such as camera shutter controls (ThinkShutter), microphone mute buttons, and privacy screen filters to enhance privacy protection and prevent unauthorized access to hardware components.

7. Application and Software Customization

- Customize software applications, productivity tools, and collaboration platforms to streamline workflows and enhance productivity. Configure application settings, keyboard shortcuts, templates, and integrations for efficient task management and collaboration.
- Use third-party customization tools, productivity add-ons, and extensions to extend functionality, automate tasks, and personalize software interfaces according to your workflow preferences.

8. Hardware Upgrades and Expansion Options

- Customize hardware configurations by upgrading RAM, storage (SSD), or adding external peripherals such as monitors, docking stations, and accessories. Upgradeable components allow users to expand storage capacity, improve multitasking performance, and connect to external devices for enhanced productivity.

- Explore advanced hardware customization options such as CPU overclocking, thermal management tweaks, and BIOS optimizations for advanced users and power users seeking maximum performance and system control.

Overall, the Lenovo ThinkPad X1 Carbon (Gen 12, 2024) provides extensive advanced customization options that empower users to tailor their computing experience, optimize system performance, and personalize hardware and software settings according to their unique needs and preferences. Whether it's fine-tuning power management, customizing keyboard shortcuts, adjusting display properties, or enhancing security features, the X1 Carbon offers flexibility and control for a personalized and efficient computing experience.

Power-user Shortcuts and Productivity Hacks

Power-user shortcuts and productivity hacks on the Lenovo ThinkPad X1 Carbon (Gen 12, 2024) enable users to work more efficiently, navigate tasks faster, and maximize productivity. These shortcuts and hacks leverage built-in features, keyboard commands, software tools, and workflow optimizations to streamline daily tasks, improve multitasking, and enhance overall user experience. Here are some power-user shortcuts and productivity hacks for the X1 Carbon:

1. Keyboard Shortcuts for Quick Actions

- Use Windows key shortcuts for common actions such as Win + E for File Explorer, Win + D for desktop view, Win + L for locking the screen, and Win + Tab for Task View. Memorize and utilize these shortcuts to navigate Windows quickly and access essential functions.

- Customize function keys (F1-F12) using Lenovo Vantage or keyboard customization software. Assign shortcuts for launching applications, switching between windows, controlling media playback, adjusting volume, and activating system settings without using mouse clicks.

2. Taskbar and Start Menu Customization

- Pin frequently used apps, folders, and documents to the taskbar or Start menu for quick access. Right-click on taskbar icons to access jump lists and recent files, enabling faster workflow navigation.
- Use the Windows Search feature (Win + S) to find files, applications, settings, and web content instantly. Utilize search filters and keyboard navigation to refine search results and locate information efficiently.

3. Multitasking and Window Management

- Use snap assist and window snapping shortcuts (Win + Arrow keys) to organize and resize windows for multitasking. Snap windows to corners or sides of the screen for split-screen views and seamless multitasking.
- Enable virtual desktops (Win + Tab) to create multiple desktop environments and separate workspaces for different tasks or projects. Switch between virtual desktops to declutter the desktop and focus on specific activities.

4. Touchpad and TrackPoint Gestures

- Learn touchpad gestures such as two-finger scrolling, pinch-to-zoom, three-finger swipe for task switching, and four-finger swipe for virtual desktops. Customize touchpad gestures in Windows settings for intuitive navigation and productivity.

- Utilize TrackPoint features for precise cursor control, text selection, and navigation without lifting your fingers from the keyboard. Combine TrackPoint movements with keyboard shortcuts for efficient workflow navigation.

5. Lenovo Vantage Productivity Tools

- Explore productivity features in Lenovo Vantage software, such as Lenovo Smart Assist, Intelligent Cooling, and Battery Optimization. Customize power modes, performance profiles, and system settings for optimal productivity and battery life.
- Use Lenovo Vantage's System Update tool to keep device drivers, BIOS, and firmware up to date. Ensure that your X1 Carbon is running the latest software versions for improved compatibility, performance, and security.

6. Application-Specific Shortcuts and Tips

- Learn application-specific keyboard shortcuts for popular productivity tools such as Microsoft Office, Adobe Creative Suite, web browsers, and email clients. Memorize common shortcuts for tasks like copy-paste, undo-redo, save, print, and format text.
- Explore advanced features and productivity hacks in software applications, such as templates, macros, automation scripts, keyboard remapping, and custom workflows. Customize application settings and preferences to align with your workflow and optimize efficiency.

7. Cloud Integration and Collaboration Tools

- Integrate cloud storage services (e.g., OneDrive, Google Drive, Dropbox) with file explorer for seamless file synchronization, backup, and sharing. Use cloud collaboration platforms (e.g., Microsoft Teams, Slack) for real-time communication, file sharing, and project collaboration.

- Explore productivity add-ons and extensions for web browsers to enhance online research, bookmarking, note-taking, and tab management. Use browser shortcuts and web tools for efficient web navigation, search, and content organization.

8. Automation and Task Management

- Implement task automation using scripting languages (e.g., PowerShell, Python) or automation tools (e.g., AutoHotkey, Task Scheduler) for repetitive tasks, batch processing, and system maintenance. Create scripts or macros to automate data entry, file operations, backups, and software updates.
- Use task management and productivity apps (e.g., Microsoft To-Do, Trello, Evernote) for organizing tasks, setting reminders, prioritizing activities, and

tracking progress. Leverage task lists, reminders, due dates, and categorization features for efficient task management and time management.

By leveraging these power-user shortcuts and productivity hacks on the Lenovo ThinkPad X1 Carbon (Gen 12, 2024), users can optimize workflow efficiency, save time on routine tasks, and enhance overall productivity and user experience. Continuous learning, practice, and customization of tools and workflows contribute to a more efficient and effective computing environment for power users and professionals alike.

Chapter 8: Frequently Asked Questions (FAQs)

Frequently Asked Questions (FAQs) provide valuable information, address common concerns, and offer solutions to potential issues that users may encounter while using the Lenovo ThinkPad X1 Carbon (Gen 12, 2024). These FAQs cover a range of topics, including hardware features, software compatibility, troubleshooting tips, and best practices for optimal usage. Here are some frequently asked questions and their answers for the X1 Carbon:

1. Q: What are the key features of the Lenovo ThinkPad X1 Carbon (Gen 12, 2024)?

A: The key features of the X1 Carbon include a lightweight and durable design, high-resolution display options, powerful Intel Core processors, long battery life, advanced security features (such as fingerprint reader and optional IR camera), and connectivity options like Thunderbolt 4 ports and Wi-Fi 6E.

2. Q: Can I upgrade the RAM and storage on the X1 Carbon?

A: The X1 Carbon (Gen 12) allows for RAM and storage upgrades. It supports up to 64GB of RAM and offers options for SSD storage upgrades. However, it's recommended to check the specific model's compatibility and consult the user manual or Lenovo's support website for detailed upgrade instructions.

3. Q: What operating system does the X1 Carbon come with? Can I install other operating systems?

A: The X1 Carbon typically comes with Windows 10 or Windows 11 pre-installed, depending on the model and configuration. However, you may be able to install other operating systems such as Linux or macOS, depending on compatibility and driver availability. Keep in mind that installing a different OS may void warranty or require additional setup steps.

4. Q: How do I enable biometric authentication (fingerprint or facial recognition) on the X1 Carbon?

A: To enable biometric authentication, go to the Windows Settings > Accounts > Sign-in options. Here, you can set up fingerprint or facial recognition authentication if your X1 Carbon model supports these features. Follow the on-screen instructions to register your biometric data and configure authentication settings.

5. Q: What should I do if my X1 Carbon is running slowly or experiencing performance issues?

A: If your X1 Carbon is running slowly, try the following troubleshooting steps:
- Close unnecessary programs and background processes.

- Update device drivers, BIOS, and firmware to the latest versions.
- Perform a disk cleanup and defragmentation.
- Adjust power settings for optimal performance.
- Consider upgrading RAM or SSD for improved performance.

6. Q: How do I connect external monitors or peripherals to the X1 Carbon?

A: The X1 Carbon features Thunderbolt 4 USB-C ports, USB-A ports, and a full-size HDMI port for connecting external monitors, peripherals, and accessories. Use compatible cables and adapters to connect monitors, keyboards, mice, printers, and other devices to the laptop. For multiple monitor setups, use Thunderbolt docking stations or USB-C hubs for expanded connectivity.

7. Q: What are some battery-saving tips for the X1 Carbon?

A: To optimize battery life on the X1 Carbon, try the following tips:

- Use power-saving modes and adjust screen brightness.
- Close background apps and disable unused hardware features.
- Keep the laptop cool and avoid prolonged exposure to high temperatures.
- Use Lenovo Vantage software to monitor battery health and optimize power settings.
- Consider using an external power bank or charger for extended usage on the go.

8. Q: How do I reset or troubleshoot my X1 Carbon if I encounter software issues?

A: If you encounter software issues on your X1 Carbon, you can try the following troubleshooting steps:

- Restart the laptop and check for updates (Windows updates, driver updates, software patches).

- Run built-in Windows troubleshooters for specific issues (e.g., network troubleshooter, hardware troubleshooter).
- Perform a system restore or reset using Windows Recovery options.
- Backup important data before performing a reset or reinstalling the operating system.
- Contact Lenovo support or consult user manuals for advanced troubleshooting and repair options.

These FAQs provide valuable insights and guidance for users of the Lenovo ThinkPad X1 Carbon (Gen 12, 2024), helping them resolve common queries, maximize functionality, and ensure a smooth user experience. For specific or detailed inquiries, users are encouraged to refer to official documentation, user manuals, support forums, and customer service resources provided by Lenovo.

Conclusion

The Lenovo ThinkPad X1 Carbon (Gen 12, 2024) is a flagship ultralight laptop that combines premium design, powerful performance, and advanced features tailored for professional users and power users. Here's a recap of the key points and features that make the X1 Carbon a standout device in its category:

1. Design and Build Quality

The X1 Carbon features a sleek and durable design with a lightweight chassis made from recycled aluminum, magnesium, aerospace-grade carbon fiber, and post-consumer materials. Its thin and elegant profile, along with a 14-inch high-resolution display (2,880 x 1,800 pixels), makes it ideal for on-the-go productivity.

2. Performance and Hardware

Powered by the latest Intel Core Ultra CPU (Ultra 7 155H chip), the X1 Carbon delivers reliable performance for multitasking, business applications, and content creation. With options for up to 64GB of RAM and SSD storage upgrades, users can experience seamless computing and faster data access.

3. Keyboard and Input Options

The X1 Carbon features Lenovo's iconic keyboard with new tactile markings for enhanced typing comfort and accuracy. Users can also take advantage of the wide touchpad, TrackPoint, and optional fingerprint reader and IR camera for secure biometric authentication and convenient input methods.

4. Connectivity and Ports

Connectivity options include Thunderbolt 4 USB-C ports (with charging support), USB-A ports, full-size HDMI port, SIM card slot (optional), Wi-Fi 6E, and Bluetooth 5.2. These ports and wireless technologies enable seamless connectivity to external monitors, peripherals, networks, and accessories.

5. Display and Graphics Performance

The X1 Carbon's OLED display offers vibrant colors, deep blacks, and crisp visuals for immersive viewing experiences. Integrated graphics and display optimizations enhance graphics performance for productivity tasks, multimedia playback, and casual gaming.

6. Battery Life and Power Management

Despite its powerful performance, the X1 Carbon maintains decent battery life, with up to nine hours of usage on a standard YouTube video playback at full brightness. Users can optimize battery life further by adjusting power settings, using power-saving modes, and monitoring battery health through Lenovo Vantage software.

7. Security and Privacy Features

Security features include a webcam with a manual shutter, fingerprint reader, IR camera for facial recognition, and optional privacy screen filters. Users can also configure passwords, encryption, and secure boot options for data protection and privacy.

The Lenovo ThinkPad X1 Carbon (Gen 12, 2024) stands out as a top choice for professionals, business users, and power users seeking a premium ultralight laptop with robust performance, innovative features, and reliable durability. Its blend of cutting-edge hardware, versatile connectivity, security enhancements, and productivity-focused design makes it a versatile tool for modern work environments. Here are some final thoughts and recommendations for potential users:

Pros

- Premium design and build quality with a lightweight and durable chassis.
- Powerful performance and multitasking capabilities for business and productivity tasks.
- Advanced security features and biometric options for secure authentication.
- Versatile connectivity options including Thunderbolt 4, Wi-Fi 6E, and Bluetooth 5.2.
- Long battery life and power management options for on-the-go productivity.

Cons

- Higher price point compared to some competitors in the ultralight laptop segment.
- Limited upgrade options for RAM and storage in certain configurations.
- Potential for thermal management challenges under heavy workloads.

Overall, the Lenovo ThinkPad X1 Carbon (Gen 12, 2024) earns high marks for its exceptional design, performance, and features, making it a recommended choice for professionals and users who prioritize productivity, mobility, and security in their computing devices. With thoughtful design elements, reliable hardware components, and a focus on user experience, the X1 Carbon delivers a premium computing experience that meets the demands of modern work and digital lifestyles.

www.ingramcontent.com/pod-product-compliance
Lightning Source LLC
LaVergne TN
LVHW051703050326
832903LV00032B/3985

ISBN 9798321603246

90000

9 798321 603246